Ireland

The Republic of Ireland, or Eire, covers an area of 70,000 square kilometers (27,000 square miles), yet has a population of only 3,500,000. Eire comprises twenty-six of all Ireland's thirty-two counties; the other six are in Northern Ireland, which is administered by the United Kingdom.

Following centuries of subjection to Britain, Ireland gained its independence in 1921, becoming a republic in 1949. Since then, the country has developed into a modern industrialized nation, exporting significant quantities of machinery, chemicals and cloth. A growth in foreign investment, particularly since Eire joined the European Economic Community in 1973, has brought jobs and prosperity to many parts of the country.

Despite Ireland's modernization, farming and fishing, the traditional occupations of the crofters, still play an important role in the economy. Vegetables, fruit, and grain are widely cultivated, and Eire's dairy products are well known throughout the world. The country's famous peat bogs provide extra income for many farmers.

Ireland has some of the finest natural scenery in Europe, attracting visitors from all corners of the world. From the Wicklow Mountains to the Kerry coast, Ireland abounds with beautiful and spectacular landscapes, which have remained remarkably unspoiled over the years.

Chris Fairclough is a freelance photographer and author who has written numerous books for children.

Northern Ireland

Irish Sea

Atlantic Ocean

Achill Island

Clifden

Connemara

Aran
Islands

The Burren

Ardara

Boyle

Shannon

Lough Corrib

Galway

Lisdoonvarna

Nenagh

Tipperary

Dingle

Cahersiveen

Killarney

Carrauntoohil

Mallow

Cork

Athlone

Ferbane

The
Curragh

Wicklow
Mountains

Waterford

Dundalk

Carrickarnon

Dublin

Arklow

Enniscorthy

Wexford

we live in IRELAND

Chris Fairclough

The Bookwright Press
New York · 1986

Living Here

We live in Argentina

We live in Australia

We live in Belgium and Luxembourg

We live in Brazil

We live in Britain

We live in Canada

We live in the Caribbean

We live in Chile

We live in China

We live in Denmark

We live in East Germany

We live in Egypt

We live in Greece

We live in France

We live in Hong Kong

We live in India

We live in Indonesia

We live in Ireland

We live in Israel

We live in Italy

We live in Japan

We live in Kenya

We live in Malaysia and Singapore

We live in Mexico

We live in the Netherlands

We live in New Zealand

We live in Pakistan

We live in the Philippines

We live in Poland

We live in Portugal

We live in Saudi Arabia

We live in South Africa

We live in Spain

We live in Sweden

We live in the U.S.A.

We live in the Asian U.S.S.R.

We live in the European U.S.S.R.

We live in West Germany

ISBN 0–531–18070–0
Library of Congress Catalog Card Number: 85–73679

First published in the United States in 1986 by
The Bookwright Press
387 Park Avenue South
New York, NY 10016

First published in 1986 by
Wayland (Publishers) Ltd
61 Western Road, Hove
East Sussex BN3 1JD, England

Phototypeset by Kalligraphics Ltd
Redhill, Surrey
Printed in Italy by G. Canale & C.S.p.A., Turin

Contents

"Turf is the traditional fuel of the Irish"

John O'Leary is 61 and lives in County Kerry. He is a crofter, working the land during the winter and fishing during the summer. He also earns extra money by cutting peat for the Electricity Supply Board.

I have spent my whole life in a tiny village called Kilpeacan Cross Roads, just south of Cahersiveen, on the west coast of Ireland. Both my father and grandfather lived here and, like me, both were crofters. My wife is a real foreigner – she comes from Wexford! I own 9 hectares (22 acres) of land, but it is split up into small strips scattered throughout the area. I use some of it for grazing and the rest for cutting turf to be burned.

In the old days, I spent most summers fishing and only worked the land during the winter or when the sea was rough. I can't manage so much fishing now, so I leave it to the younger men. It's not as it used to be, anyway, what with all the foreign boats that come here now.

My land is very spread out, so I have to use the main road when I move my cattle from one pasture to another. Although the road is a popular route with the tourists, they don't seem to mind waiting for the cows. In fact, they seem to enjoy it. You would think that some of them had never

John moves his cattle from one pasture to another along the main road.

seen a cow before, the way they "ooh" and "aah" and point!

Just up the road at Cahersiveen, the Electricity Supply Board has recently built the largest peat-burning power station in Eire. Most of the local crofters now cut peat, or "turf," as we call it, for the station. Some use highly expensive cutting machines, but the rest of us still follow the age-old method of cutting by hand. My son and I cut about 100 tons a year between us. The money we get for the peat helps to supplement the income we receive from raising cows.

Turf is the traditional fuel of the Irish, as we have no coal to speak of in this country. Blocks of wet turf are cut from the bogs that cover about one-fifth of the total land area of Eire. These are then stacked up to allow the air to dry them, before they are removed to the cottages for burning. Digging turf is a hard and back-breaking job, but for centuries it has been a way of life here on the west coast.

Crofters traditionally lived in low, thatched cottages, but these are fast disappearing now. The EEC has brought new-found wealth to the west coast and new houses of brick are being built all over the place. It's sad to see the traditional ways die, but that's progress, and we have been saved from it for a long time now. Nevertheless, sitting in a centrally-heated house, eating sliced bread out of a packet isn't quite the same as watching a batch of dough rise in the corner of a turf-warmed hearth. It's convenient, I'll give you that, but the bread will never taste half as good.

For centuries the Irish have dug turf to be burned as fuel.

"Connemara is covered with lakes"

Tom Molloy was born in 1928. After working in London for a while, he returned to Oughterard, in Connemara, in 1956. Since then, he has worked as a boatman, taking fishermen out to the best fishing grounds in his boat.

I was brought up here on the shores of Lough Corrib in Connemara, County Galway. My father was a boatman and he taught me a great deal of what I know today. The ways of the world may have changed, but the habits of the fish certainly haven't. All my father knew counts for as much today as it did fifty years ago. Connemara is that area of Galway that is covered with lakes. Everywhere you go there is water; some fresh and running with trout, some salt and running with salmon. Sometimes you have to taste the water just to tell the difference.

In 1949 I left this land of rock and water

Tom sets off with a customer for another day's fishing.

The traditional boats Tom rows are made by local craftsmen.

and went to London. I got a job working for the telephone companies, putting in junction boxes. I found London fascinating, but eventually I grew homesick for the sound of oars straining in rowlocks and the hum of the mayfly hatch in the warmth of the late afternoon sunshine. I had been brought up in Connemara and it was only when I went away that I realized how much it was a part of my life. I've been back now since 1956 and have no desire to ever leave again.

I earn my living by "showing the way." I'm the middle man between the fisherman and the fish. People hire my services by the day, week or month. I take them out in my boat to a spot where I think they are likely to catch a fish. Sometimes they fish on their own, but I often join them. Most of my clients come from West Germany, Britain, France and Holland, although there was a time when about ninety percent of them were members of the English upper class. Fishing has also become a local sport now – gone are the days when we were there simply to row the boats and doff our caps.

There are three main methods of fishing here: using metal spinners or lures; trolling with an artificial fly on the surface of the lough; and thirdly, dapping with a real mayfly. During the mayfly season, the local boys catch the flies and sell them to the fishermen. The mayfly season, which lasts from mid-May to early June, is the best time for good catches of trout. After that, most fish are caught using lures, especially spoon baits trolled slowly through the water.

The local hotels are very helpful to the boatmen, and the tourists. They put them in touch with each other, thus providing a service for their clients and a source of income for us boatmen.

The fish are not as easy to catch these days, and often we return in the evenings with only a couple for the pan. But what better way is there to end the day than to sit enjoying the taste of fresh trout and Irish whiskey, while planning the next day's fishing.

"We all have to learn Irish"

Maria Lahiff is 8 and lives near Boyle, in County Roscommon, where her parents own and run a lakeside restaurant. She attends a first-level (elementary) school in Boyle, where she is taught a variety of subjects, including Irish.

I live with my brother, Peter, and our parents in Lough Key Forest Park, near Boyle, County Roscommon. Mum and Dad run a restaurant here on the lakeside for all the people who visit the park. It's a wonderful place to visit, but when you actually live in the park, it's even better. Peter and I are always exploring the forest and the lakeside. We are friends with one of the local boatmen, and he often rows us to a castle which stands on an island in the middle of the lough.

Lough Key Forest Park covers about 350 hectares (865 acres) of the Lough Key Forest, one of the 253 state forests in Eire. The forest is full of beautiful broad-leaved trees, but there are some giant cedars and conifers too. The park is criss-crossed by paths and tracks which my brother and I like to explore, all the time watching out for stoats, deer, hedgehogs, badgers, otters and red squirrels.

When we are not in the park or helping our parents in the restaurant, we have to go to school. All children in Eire have to go to school when they are 6, and must stay on until they are 15. Peter and I go to a first-level school. These are for children between the ages of 6 and 12. Nearly all of them are run by the state. There are about 580,000 children at first-level schools in Eire, which is about fifteen per-

Many children rely on the school bus to get them to their classes.

cent of the total population. Most of our schools are Catholic. For the first year the classes are mixed, but after that boys go to one school and girls to another.

We stay in the same classroom all day and have the same teacher for most of our lessons. There are special classes for slow-learning children and those from itinerant families. My favorite subject is math, but I like reading and writing too. We all have to learn Irish, but I'm not as good at it as Peter. He can read Irish books and once won a prize for writing a story in the Irish language. Irish is a compulsory subject in most schools.

School begins at 9:20 a.m. every morning. Some children catch a school bus, but Peter and I walk. As soon as we get to the classroom, we all say a prayer for the day, and then our first lesson begins. This is usually Irish. Lunch is at 12:30, but we only get half an hour to eat our sandwiches. School finishes at 3:00 p.m., and we usually get about an hour's homework.

Next year, when Peter is 12, he will go to secondary school. He's quite bright, so he should have no trouble getting his intermediate certificate when he is 15. If he stays on at school, he'll then take his leaving certificate (high school diploma) at 17 before going to university in Dublin. He wants to teach languages, but I would rather stay here in the forest and help Mum and Dad in the restaurant.

The beautiful scenery of Lough Key attracts many visitors.

"More than 1.7 million papers are sold a week"

Michael Foley is 34. Having spent some years working in England, he returned to Ireland in 1977 to take up a job as a staff reporter with *The Irish Times*, one of the country's four national newspapers. His special subject is tourism.

I have spent the last nine years writing for *The Irish Times*, one of the four daily national newspapers printed in Eire. Three of them – *The Irish Times*, *The Irish Press* and *The Irish Independent* – are published in Dublin, and the other is *The Cork Examiner*. Ireland has one of the highest newspaper readerships in the whole of Europe: more than 1.7 million national papers are sold a week. There are also more than eighty regional dailies and weeklies, the most popular being *The Kerryman*. Many of these provincial newspapers are family concerns which still use the old hot-metal methods of production.

Michael checks the "paste-up" of an article which he has written for the newspaper.

The head office of The Irish Times *is located in the busy center of Dublin.*

All the national dailies, however, use modern phototypesetting methods, taking advantage of the new computer technology. *The Cork Examiner* has probably the most modern newspaper production system in Europe.

When I'm not working specifically for the newspaper's tourism section, I join the other reporters in the courts or the parliament buildings. We have only a small staff of about 130 people, so each of us has to cover stories that are outside our own particular fields of speciality. Like most papers in Eire, we cover the news in Irish as well as English. Every week at least three columns of the paper are in Gaelic.

The Irish language is also well represented on radio and television. We have one broadcasting service, called *Radio Telefis Eiraan* (RTE), which runs Ireland's two television channels, RTE 1 and RTE 2. Together they transmit about 100 hours of television every week. About forty percent of this is made up of home-produced current affairs, drama, light entertainment, sport, education and farming programs, some in Irish and some in English. The remaining sixty percent of programs are imported, mostly from the United States and Britain.

RTE broadcasts radio programs on three different channels. RTE 1 and 2 are very mixed in their programming, whereas *Radio na Gaeltachta* is an all-Irish service, mainly serving those people who live in the *Gaeltachta* districts.

When I'm not working, I like to go to the movies. Our film industry has slowly been growing over the last few years. Our film-makers tend to look to Australia for inspiration, because that country has recently produced some fine films on very low budgets. Irish locations are often used by film companies and everybody must have seen *Ryan's Daughter* and *The Blue Max*, both shot in this country by Irish film crews. Our most recent success was *Cal*, a film about the troubles in Northern Ireland, which was popular with both the public and the critics. That is a rare feat in the film world.

"The feeling of belonging is fast disappearing"

Patrick Lawlee is 74 and lives in Mallow, County Cork. He retired from his job at a sugar beet processing plant in 1976. He now spends most of his time painting his house, which has become something of a tourist attraction.

My grandfather had this house built in 1884 and he lived here until he died. When I got married in 1935, my wife and I moved in and made it our home. I worked on a farm then, but the wages were terrible, so when I got the chance to work for the post office I jumped at it. That job didn't last very long though, and I ended up laboring on the railways for the next six summers.

By that time we had a couple of children, so I couldn't go on with such an insecure job. I applied for a position in the local sugar refining factory and was accepted. A good deal of sugar is produced here in County Cork, much of it for export. I worked in that factory for forty years, so I was glad to retire in 1976.

Now I get a retirement pension from the Department of Social Welfare. Both men and women retire at 66, when they are entitled to an allowance based on the obligatory and voluntary contributions they have made during their lives. It's a complicated system and I don't think any-

one really understands it, but my wife and I do all right and don't want for much. As pensioners, we get free bus travel, television licences and medical treatment, as well as vouchers entitling us to cheap electricity and fuel.

Patrick fears Mallow's beautiful scenery could be harmed by modern farming methods.

I spend most of my time painting – not pictures, but my house. It was the first thing I did when I retired, and since then it has become quite a hobby with me. I don't do murals or anything, I just like the house to look bright and clean. I paint everything inside and out; I've even painted the chimney. Something I have always wanted to do is to paint all the tiles on the roof different colors, but I think I may be getting a bit too old to spend the whole day up on a ladder.

People from all over the world have stopped to take photos of my house or just to have a chat. A German has even made a postcard of my house and I've appeared in two books about Ireland. In fact, I'm

Patrick's painted house has become well known in Ireland.

getting to be quite a celebrity!

For every car that stops outside my house, there must be a thousand that rush straight past. The streets are narrow and bendy, but still the motorists speed through the village. People today seem to have different priorities to those of my generation. Everything has to be faster and bigger than the next man's, whereas in my day we all worked hard and then went for a drink and a chat in the evening. We used to live together as a community, but that feeling of belonging is fast disappearing, even here in the country.

"I praise God for creating such a landscape"

Sister Mary is the headmistress of the Kylemore Abbey School near Clifden, in Connemara, County Galway. She has lived at the abbey since 1937, when she first came to the school as a pupil.

I was born in County Galway and came to school here at Kylemore Abbey when I was 12 years old. After my initial education, I took my vows and became a Benedictine nun. I also promised to stay at Kylemore for the rest of my life. I soon became a teacher here and have been headmistress for the last 12 years.

We take about a hundred boarders and up to eighty day pupils at the school. Five of our nuns teach, although there are more than thirty nuns in our community as a whole. We also employ a further ten lay teachers. Our classes follow the syllabus laid down by the Irish Department of Education and we teach all subjects, including, of course, Christian doctrine and liturgy.

About ninety-three percent of the people who live in the Irish Republic are Catholics. The remainder are Protestants (either Church of Ireland, Presbyterian or

A statue of the Virgin Mary at the roadside – a common sight in Ireland.

Methodist) or people with no specific religious belief.

Ireland was converted to Christianity in the fifth century by St. Patrick, who is now the patron saint of Ireland. During the sixteenth century, the Protestant Church of Ireland became the country's official Church, but it was forced upon the Irish by the English Tudor kings. Catholicism went underground and it wasn't until 1892 that the full civil rights of Irish Catholics were recognized.

The Catholic Church is organized on an all-Ireland basis, taking in both Northern Ireland and Eire. It is split into four ecclesiastical regions, each headed by an archbishop. The Archbishop of Armagh, which is in Northern Ireland, is the Primate of All Ireland.

Although many people today seem unable to accept everything the Church stands for, a large number of them continue to practice the religion. There are over 18,000 men and women in Ireland's various Catholic orders of nuns, brothers and priests. We also send missionaries to many countries, including those in the Third World.

When I was younger, I used to climb to the top of some of the mountains in this area. These days I haven't the energy to go hiking, but each morning I praise God for creating such a majestical landscape for us to enjoy. The mountains change color and mood so quickly: one minute they are dark and forboding, with heavy mists rolling down their sides, and the next moment the sun shines across the peaks, making them seem calm and serene. The sight of their reflection in the lake on a May morning is enough to help me through even the busiest of days without a rest.

Kylemore Abbey is surrounded by magnificent natural landscapes.

"Ireland is famous for its 'praities'"

James Lennon is 52. He is married and has five sons. He owns a farm and rents some extra land in County Roscommon. He grows vegetables which he sells every week in his local market at Ballinasloe.

We live near Athlone, northwest of the Bog of Allan and just north of the Shannon River. Athlone is at the southern end of Lough Ree and it takes its name from an innkeeper who once lived here. His name was Luan and the river ford near his inn was known as Ath Luan – Athlone. The Shannon River was always the dividing line between eastern and western Ireland and there have been many battles fought at Athlone.

Some of those battles were probably fought on my land. I own 9 hectares (23 acres) and rent another 8 hectares (20 acres) from other people in the area. We have high-quality peat soil here which doesn't need much irrigation, even in the driest months. This sort of land is very expensive to buy these days; I couldn't afford to buy any more, but I go to the auctions anyway, just to see what my small farm is worth. Currently 1 hectare

The peat soil of the Athlone area is ideal for growing vegetables.

18

(2½ acres) of flat bog costs about I£6,200 ($7,800).

I grow mostly carrots, turnips, cabbages and potatoes. Once a week my wife and I "bag up" all the produce and price it. Modern housewives like the vegetables to be sold in bags; that way it does not get their shopping baskets dirty. The following day I sell the produce on my market-stall in Ballinasloe.

Most of my days are spent in the fields. When you grow vegetables, there is always something to do. It is not like growing a huge field of wheat, where you just wait for it to grow before harvesting it. With vegetables you are always plowing or digging or spraying. Because I sell my own produce, I have to avoid having a glut of vegetables at any one time. I therefore have to harvest the rows of carrots at different times. It's no good me planting all my carrots together, because they would then all be ready for market the same week.

I only grow a few potatoes here, although Ireland is famous for its "praities." In the past, the country was almost totally dependent on the potato crop; during the potato famine of 1846 and 1847, 2 million people starved to death. Most Irish potatoes are now grown in County Donegal or away up on the coast north of Dublin.

Here in the middle of Ireland, the land is fairly flat and we do not have the dramatic scenery they have in, say, County Galway. But we do have one tourist attraction in this area, and that is the Shannon River. In recent years, there has been a growing interest in hiring cruisers on the river, which, at 380 km (240 miles) in length, is the longest river in the British Isles. I would like to take a holiday on the river, but I couldn't afford to be away from home for that long. After all, who would look after my vegetables?

Potatoes are still harvested by hand in many parts of Ireland.

"We Irish love an audience"

Gillian Wilkinson is 30. She works in Dublin as a computer programmer and analyst, but her first love is music. She sings in pubs and clubs all over Eire and is also a member of the Abbey Tavern Singers.

My mother was English and my father Irish. Both were good singers and our house was always full of music. Singing has been my only hobby since I was 4 years old.

Gillian and some other members of the Abbey Tavern Singers performing to a packed house.

I spend my days as a programmer and analyst for a multinational computer company in Dublin. Many foreign companies have set up offices or factories in Eire during the past twenty years, taking advantage of a willing workforce and govern-

A landscape in County Kerry – the home of traditional Irish music.

ment incentives for new businesses. The EEC has also encouraged investment.

My singing takes me all over Eire during my vacation and on weekends. On some weekday evenings, I sing with a local group called the Abbey Tavern Singers. The Abbey Tavern is a well-known "music pub" in Howth, a suburb of Dublin. About sixteen performers make up the Abbey Tavern Singers, although there are only seven of us on stage at any one time. Most of us are singers, but the group also has four full-time musicians: two fiddlers, an accordionist and a bodhran-player.

A bodhran is a type of drum which is very popular in Cork and Kerry. It is made by stretching a goatskin over a thin, circular wooden frame and is played with a double-ended drumstick held between the finger and thumb. It looks a bit like a tamborine without the bells. Other instruments associated with Irish music are the Irish bagpipes, the tin whistle, the guitar and the harp although the latter is rarely played these days.

Each area in Ireland has its own style of music. Most of the tunes have been written down by performers and collectors over the years, but new songs and ballads are always turning up. Singers come from every walk of life and from every corner of the country.

Although Irish music is just one of many forms of entertainment today, it played a far greater role in the lives of our predecessors, for whom it was the only means of amusement. The poet, or bard, was in medieval times the most highly respected man in the community. The Irish music tradition stems from the medieval poets and it is them we have to thank for our rich musical heritage.

All the songs were, of course, written and performed in Gaelic. We sometimes still sing in Irish, but as most of our audiences cannot understand the language, many of our songs, and the ballads in particular, have been translated into English.

You don't have to go to an organized event to hear Irish music: just walk through any village at sunset and you will be bound to hear singing coming from some house or other. Knock at the door and the chances are you'll be invited in – we Irish love an audience.

21

"Every vote cast has an effect on the outcome"

Maurice Manning is 42. He is a TD (Teachdaí Dála), the name given to a member of the Irish Parliament. He belongs to Fine Gael, which together with the Labour Party, forms the present coalition government in Ireland.

The Republic of Ireland is an independent sovereign state. It came into existence in 1922 after the Anglo-Irish Treaty of 1921. This treaty conceded dominion status within the British Commonwealth to the twenty-six counties that made up the Irish Free State.

The early years of the Irish Free State saw a great deal of turmoil, with civil war breaking out between those who upheld the treaty and those who didn't. In 1937, Eamon De Valera, the leader of the then ruling Fianna Fáil party, introduced a new constitution which abolished the name Irish Free State. In its place, Eire (Ireland) was declared an independent sovereign nation, with a president as head of state. It officially became a republic in 1949.

The President of Ireland is elected by the people. Every citizen over 35 is eligible to stand for president, and everyone over 18 can vote. The term of office is seven years and each president can only be re-elected once. The president is the head of state and the official guardian of the constitution. Although he or she appoints the prime minister (taoiseach), most of the president's actions and decisions are made on the advice of the government. Before each bill becomes law it must have the president's signature, and he alone has the right to summon or dissolve Dáil

Every Irish citizen over the age of 18 has the right to vote.

Maurice chats to one of his local constituents outside the Dáil.

Éireann, the lower house of the legislature, although he would only do this on the advice of the government.

The present Dáil Éireann has 166 members, called (TDs) Teachdaí Dála, of which I am one. Together with Seanad Éireann (The Irish Senate), which has 60 members, and the President, we make up the Oireachtas (National Parliament).

Members of Dáil Éireann are elected by a national secret ballot. There are forty-three constituencies in Ireland and each one returns at least three members to Dáil Éireann. They are all elected by proportional representation, using a single transferable vote system. This ensures that every vote cast in an election has an effect on the outcome. Of the 166 members of Dáil Éireann, 16 are women, which is the highest proportion in any parliament in Western Europe outside Denmark.

There are four main political parties in Ireland. I am a member of Fine Gael, which, with the Labour Party, forms the present coalition government. The other two parties are Fianna Fáil and the Workers' Party; the latter is also represented in Northern Ireland.

My job as a TD is very insecure. There could be an election tomorrow and I might not be re-elected. I am, however, lucky in that I have a profession to fall back on — I'm a lecturer in politics at University College, Dublin. Therefore, when I'm not dealing with affairs of state myself, I spend my time telling others how it should be done!

"Above all, visitors come for the flowers"

Maryangela Keane is 51. She and her family run a small hotel in Lisdoonvarna, County Clare. She is a leading authority on the Burren, the unique geographical region in which Lisdoonvarna is situated.

Our hotel has been in the family for over one hundred years. My daughter, Melissa, is one of the fifth generation to have worked here. This is a small family hotel, like many others in Eire, in which we try to provide a home from home for our maximum of twenty guests. We have a small restaurant, too, serving food from a nearby farm which we also own.

Lisdoonvarna is a small town in the region called the Burren. The Burren occupies an area of about 900 sq km (350 sq miles) in the west of County Clare, south of Galway Bay. It is the youngest landscape in the whole of Europe, having undergone glaciation only 15,000 years ago. There is now only limestone in this area, and all the typical limestone formations, such as subterranean streams, swallow holes, and limestone caves, can be seen here.

Before people first came to the Burren

Maryangela and her daughter help some guests plan a walking vacation.

24

about 5,000 years ago, the area was covered with pine forest. Extensive farming stripped the landscape of vegetation, however, and it is now one vast expanse of bare rock and windswept hillsides. When Cromwell's army invaded Ireland, one of the English generals, Ludlow, commented that the Burren had "not enough earth to bury a man, not enough wood to hang him, nor enough water to drown him." Things have changed little since that time.

This strange and dramatically beautiful landscape now attracts people from all over the world. They come to see the bare hills, to visit the many wedge-shaped burial chambers that our ancestors left us, and to walk among the ruins of the hundreds of churches scattered throughout the region. But above all, visitors come for the flowers. The Burren is unique in its variety of flowers, some of which are extremely rare and are seen nowhere else in the world. Species of plant that are generally considered to dislike limestone are even found here.

The reasons why the flowers thrive are threefold: firstly, the Gulf Stream brings warm, moist air into this area; secondly, the light is very strong due to reflections from sea and rock; and thirdly, the limestone absorbs a great deal of heat into the soil. During the winter, the hills in the Burren are warmer than the valleys, so the farmers are able to leave their cattle out on the hills throughout the year.

At our hotel, we specialize in providing holidays for people interested in flowers. We have our own natural history library, and I spend a great deal of my day chatting to guests, drawing maps for them, and generally helping them plan their stay to take in all the flowers that are blooming.

The Burren's distinctive landscape makes it a popular destination.

"Physiotherapy and chest X rays are free to all"

Mary O'Keefe is married and has a son. She works as a physiotherapist in the out-patients department of a small local hospital in Nenagh, County Tipperary. When she is not busy at the hospital, she likes to play golf.

I work in a small local hospital with 100 beds. We have a staff of seventy nurses, two surgeons, two physicians and one and a half physiotherapists! There is not enough money to pay for two full-time phystiotherapists, so I work only three hours each morning, five days a week. I enjoy the job because I am always dealing with a broad cross section of the local community: one hour I might be helping to rehabilitate an accident victim and the next hour I might be encouraging an athlete to get his or her muscles working again after an operation.

Everyone in Ireland is entitled to free health care, although there are a few provisos. People on the lowest incomes, and all those over 66 and under 18, are issued with a medical card. This entitles them to free doctor's appointments, hospitalization and, in some cases, free dental and optical treatment. About forty percent of the population fall into this category.

Those who are in full-time employment, but who don't earn over I£12,500 ($15,760) a year, get free hospital care but must pay for certain other services like going to see their GPs (general practitioners) at their surgeries (doctor's offices). This costs about I£7 ($8.80) a visit. People who earn over I£12,500 ($15,760) get free hospital care but must pay for everything else. However, physiotherapy and chest X rays are free to all.

There are 1,400 doctors in Eire and each one is responsible for about 1,000 people. They have both private and public patients and work on a contractual basis for the health service. Some hospitals are run by private organizations, including the Roman Catholic Church, but most of them are funded by the state.

It is very difficult to enter the medical profession in Ireland. You have to be bright and very hard-working. A friend of mine tried to train as a nurse at practically every hospital in the country, but could not get taken on. Eventually, she had to go to England to take up her chosen career.

I am a married woman, which means

Ireland's health service is funded by the government through eight regional boards.

that before 1972 I would have had to give up my career after my marriage, because no married women were allowed to practice a profession in the public services in Ireland. That has all changed now, of course, and many Irish women go on working after marriage.

On weekends and when I have some time during the week, I like to play golf. Nenagh has an excellent eighteen-hole course, one of the 250 throughout Eire. The sport is becoming increasingly popular in this country, and our professional players are now starting to build international reputations for themselves.

Irish golf courses have become internationally famous.

"Our industry is unique to Ireland"

Billy Flynn is a shift supervisor at the Ferbane Generating Station in County Offaly. Ferbane is one of the seven peat-fueled power stations currently in operation in Eire.

I've been working here at Ferbane since 1953, although the station didn't start to produce electricity until 1957. When I started here, I worked as a steel fixer on the two cooling towers. Each one is over 80 m (260 ft) high and now more than 18 million liters (4 million gallons) of water circulate through them every hour. When the towers were complete, I applied to work for the Electricity Supply Board and have been here ever since.

We burn 2,500 tons of milled peat every day at Ferbane. It all comes from the 5,000 hectares (12,500 acres) of workable bog-land that surround the station. The Irish have used peat as a domestic fuel for centuries, but it is only recently that this huge natural resource has been tapped to generate electricity.

Peat bogs cover about one-sixth of the total surface of Eire. Before peat can be burned, the bogs have to be thoroughly drained. Undeveloped bog is about ninety percent water, so the digging of drainage channels and ditches is a laborious job. Once it has been done, a layer of peat about 2 cm thick is scraped off the surface of the drained bog and left in the sun to dry. This is then turned and harrowed before being loaded into railway wagons, in which it is taken to the power station.

The railway wagons are brought right

Digging peat for power stations has become a good source of employment.

Rich peat farmland surrounds Ferbane Power Station.

into the power station, where the peat is unloaded into a huge hopper. This is connected by conveyor belts to several different storage hoppers. When the peat is required to be burned, it is simply dropped into the furnaces. Electricity here is generated at 10,000 volts and is then transformed to 110,000 volts, prior to being fed into the national grid. Milled peat costs about I£17 ($21) a ton, compared to I£180 ($227) a ton for fuel oil. At less than one-tenth the cost of fuel oil, peat is an extremely economical energy source.

The Irish Peat Development Board (*Bord na Mona*) was set up in 1946 to oversee the use of peat, both as a fuel and as an aid to horticulture. Since then, it has developed more than 80,000 hectares (200,000 acres) of bog. The topmost layer of peat in any bog is useless for power production; it is too fibrous and light. These qualities, however, make it ideal as a soil conditioner and aerator. Unlike fuel peat, which is sold exclusively in Ireland, about ninety percent of our agricultural peat is exported.

All in all, this is a very interesting and challenging place to work. The men here are dedicated to their jobs and are proud to work in our industry, which is unique to Ireland. Over the years, I have watched this station take shape and develop into the efficient unit it is today, so I hope that it continues to provide electricity for many years to come.

"Mares want for nothing while at the Curragh"

Ciaran Dunne is 18. For the last few months, he has worked as a student manager at the Irish National Stud in Tully, County Kildare. He is responsible for feeding the horses and for cleaning out the stables.

This stud farm was given to the British by its one-time owner, Colonel Hall-Walker, in 1915. He had bred many fine horses here and wanted the facilities he had created to be donated to the nation. The farm was eventually handed over to the Irish Government in 1943, and two years later the Irish National Stud was born.

Our role is to help breeders, both Irish and foreign, by managing the breeding of their mares with our first-class stallions. We also experiment with different ways of housing, feeding and generally looking

The flat, soft, ground of the Curragh makes it a popular location with horse trainers.

after horses.

Horses are very much a part of people's lives here in the Curragh, a 20 square-kilometer area of drained bog that has become the home of Irish racing. The Irish Derby is always run on the Curragh Racecourse, just down the road from here.

My day begins at 7:00 a.m., when I walk round the stables and help check that all the horses are fit and well. We have up to 400 mares here at any one time, so that is no small job. Then all the straw has to be replaced, before the mares and foals are let out into the paddocks at 9:00 a.m.

We have seven resident stallions here at the stud. We also have twenty-four brood mares which are sometimes used for breeding. All the other mares here are owned by private breeders. The owners are charged for each "serving" by a stallion; how much they are charged depends on the value of the horse. The lowest fee would be about I£3,000 ($3,780) and the most expensive I£15,000 ($18,900). For this money, the breeder gets the very best for his mare, including daily visits from the vet, first-class accommodation and, above all, the combined experience of some of the top people in the livestock business in Ireland. The mares want for nothing while at the Curragh.

By midday, all the "servings" are complete. I then mix the feed and give it to the animals, before bringing the mares back inside. A final sweep of the yards at 5:00 p.m. and that's my day finished.

I was one of 350 applicants from all over the world who tried to enlist on this six-month course. The stud can only accept 30 trainees, so I was lucky. Courses in stud management begin in January each year. At the end of the course, the stud helps us to find a job, although it's usually away from the Curragh. I'm hoping to go to the United States for about two years. When I get back, I'll still be young enough to be able to pick and choose the exact job I want. I rather fancy working for a bloodstock agency, buying and selling horses for breeding. Whatever I do, I know that it will be something to do with horses, so I am sure to enjoy it. Even if I am mucking out stables for another two years, I won't mind. Nevertheless, I'm aiming higher than that!

When he leaves the Curragh, Ciaran hopes to work abroad.

"The brewery uses 9 million liters of water a day"

Peter Walsh is 38. He has worked for Guinness for the past sixteen years, first in management and now as the curator of the Guinness Museum in Dublin. The museum was founded in 1966 and now attracts 50,000 visitors a year.

The word Guinness has become synonymous with two things: Ireland and stout. This company, now famous throughout the world as the leading brewer of Irish stout, began its long and well-documented history in 1759. In that year, Arthur Guinness, then 34, set up a brewery at St.James Gate, next to the Liffey River in Dublin. He signed a 9,000 year lease on the site, at a cost of £45 a year. The brewery still occupies the same site, although it has now expanded to cover 26 hectares (65 acres). It is stocked with some of the most modern brewing equipment in the world and uses 9 million liters (2 million gallons) of water a day.

By 1799, the brewery was already a great success and Arthur had been Master of the Corporation of Brewers for thirty years. He then made the most important decision in the history of the brewery: he decided to make only stout, or porter, as it was called, because of its popularity with the porters at Covent Garden Market who favored its strong and bitter taste.

Arthur Guinness died in 1803, leaving the running of the brewery to his son, also called Arthur. At the time of his father's death, "Arthur II" was a successful banker (he went on to become Governor of the Bank of Ireland in 1820), but he still found

The brewery site covers 64 acres of land in the center of Dublin.

time to make the Guinness brewery the largest and most successful in Ireland. Like his father, he had a benevolent attitude towards the people of Dublin and made many generous donations towards the upkeep of buildings and the provision of parks and housing.

Arthur Guinness II was succeeded at the helm of the Guinness empire by his son, Benjamin Lee, who took Guinness from being the largest brewery in Ireland to being the largest in the world. He became Lord Mayor of Dublin in 1851 and, like his predecessors, used his position to effect many public works. His greatest gift to Dublin was the funding of the restoration of St. Patrick's Cathedral at a cost of £150,000.

The word "museum" usually conjures up visions of Victorian glass cases and dark oak tables. Our museum is not at all like that. It is full of modern visual aids and involves a good deal of participation on the part of the visitors. This, we hope, makes the museum a far more interesting place. I believe a curator should be an educator first and an academic second. He or she should help visitors experience the past, using the props of modern technology. People seem to like this type of museum; by the end of 1987, we hope to have doubled the 50,000 visitors we now get every year. With good advertising, we aim to make this museum as famous as our stout, of which 9 million glasses are sold every day in 140 countries throughout the world.

Guinness uses the most advanced brewing techniques available.

"We must encourage more investment"

Joe Leacy is 36. He and his brother run a building company in Enniscorthy, County Wexford. They used to build a number of private houses, but now most of their work is undertaken for the local authority.

I served my apprenticeship with a couple of building companies here in Enniscorthy, a fairly large market town north of Wexford. Enniscorthy is on the Slaney River, at the head of the navigable water. In days gone by, sailing ships from all around the world would come up here to ply their trade. That is now history, and the only reminder of that time is Enniscorthy Castle, which used to guard the river.

Having served our apprenticeships, my brother and I decided to get together and start our own construction business.

We now employ two men full time, but a few years ago, we were employing as many as six. Most of the houses we build are for the local authority; in fact, we've only built three private houses in the past three years.

The building of council houses in Ireland is handled by the local authorities. They are responsible for providing houses

The Wicklow Mountains are a favorite retreat for town-dwellers.

A quarter of all new houses in Ireland are built for local authorities.

for those most in need.

Since the 1950s, large numbers of people have been flocking into the cities from the country. Now more than half of Eire's people live in urban areas. This has entailed a large building program, with new estates going up around most of the large towns and cities. Currently about twenty-five percent of all homes are built for local authorities, although in our area the percentage is higher, because few people have enough money to buy a home or to rent privately.

County Wexford has been hit very hard by unemployment. Unemployment in Ireland is running at about seventeen percent, six percent over the European average, but here in Enniscorthy it is as high as thirty percent. It is not unusual for us to build twenty houses on an estate (a development) and then find that only two of the households have a working member.

What we need in Wexford is an influx of foreign business. In other parts of Ireland, large overseas companies have set up business and the job situation has eased overnight. Since 1960, there has been about I£7,500 ($9,400 million) invested in Ireland by foreign companies, but this is still not enough. We must encourage more investment if we are ever to escape from the curse of unemployment and the apathy that it creates among the young.

About 12km north of Enniscorthy are the Wicklow Mountains. Like many other people who live in the town, I like to take my family there on holidays and at weekends. There are many paths and tracks through the mountains and one day we might even climb to the top of Lugnaquillia, which at 926m (3,037ft) is the highest peak in the Wicklow Mountains.

"We make 225 different styles of sweaters"

Imelda Boyd is 28 and lives in County Donegal with her husband. She works as a machine knitter for John Molloy, a well-known and successful weaving and knitwear manufacturer in Ardara.

I have worked for John Molloy for the last seven years. Our company is only one of many weaving and knitwear concerns based in Ardara, a town in Donegal that has grown up around the industry.

The company was founded in 1930, when John Molloy, who still works here, began employing local weavers to make his designs by hand. By 1950, the company was well established and the quality of our product had become renowned throughout the world. During the mid-Sixties, however, the textile industry went into recession and John took on a number of knitters to supplement the dwindling trade in woven materials.

By 1975, the company was well on the way back to full production, and John Molloy now employs more than 2,500 hand-knitters from nine counties throughout Eire. They work in their own homes, where they are supplied with wool each month. They are paid according to how many garments they have produced at the end of the month.

John Molloy's factory in Ardara employs eighty machine knitters.

We only produce five styles of hand-knit sweaters, and they are all made with white wool. It is impossible for this company to survive solely on its income from hand-knits, so in 1979 knitting machines were introduced to supplement the hand-made garments. This proved a most successful expansion and now I am one of eighty people employed to operate the machines in the Ardara factory.

We make 225 different styles of sweaters by machine, mostly in pastel colors. The company is extremely aware of fashion trends in different parts of the world, and in the United States in particular.

Because we use only the very highest quality wool, a lot of it has to be imported from Australia and New Zealand. Irish wool tends to be too coarse and the fibers are very short. This did not matter so much in the past, when continuity of style and shape were not imperative, but on today's ever-changing fashion scene, we need a constantly high standard of material.

Donegal is famous for its hand-woven tweed. In the past, it was usually the men who did the weaving. They would work the land and fish for six months and then sit at their looms for the next six months. Weaving is a difficult job and it's very hard to learn. You can't pick it up overnight: it takes years of practice. The loom has to tick regularly and it is this rhythm that gives each weaver his own "handwriting" – his own particular style of weaving.

When I'm not working in the factory, I like to walk along the Donegal cliffs. To the south of Ardara is Slieve League, the highest peak of a range of mountains that run along the Donegal coast. It is a long climb to the top, but once you are there, you can look down on the rolling hills of Donegal and out across the Atlantic Ocean. I am sure if it were just a little less misty, you would be able to see America!

Weaving has traditionally been a man's job in Ireland.

"The future of Carnmore looks very exciting"

John Clarke, 50, is a qualified pilot. He comes from Rochdale in Lancashire, England, but has lived in Ireland since 1969. For the last twelve years, he has worked at Carnmore Airport, just outside Galway, where he is now the airport manager.

After completing my national service with the RAF in 1957, I started working for Woolworth's in Manchester. I enjoyed the job, but in 1969 I was given the opportunity to set up a distributing company in Ireland. My mother came from Ireland, so, I had no hesitation in taking the job. I had done a fair amount of flying in my RAF days, but it was only when I came over to Ireland that I took up flying again, obtaining my private pilot's license in 1971 and my instructor's ticket in 1973.

The distributing company folded in 1974 and I took up a position with a German company called Steiner. They make metalized film for use in the production of capacitors, of which they are the largest manufacturers in the world. Their Irish factory is located just outside Galway at a place called Carnmore.

' In those days, Mr. Steiner was a keen aviator. He owned his own plane, which he used to travel between Germany and the Irish factory. He kept the plane on a small airfield, called Oranmore, near the

factory, but unfortunately Oranmore was a grass strip, so it couldn't be used in the winter. This annoyed Mr. Steiner, so he had a tarmac strip built next to the factory, together with a hangar for his plane. It was then that he offered me the job of looking after the runway and overseeing the maintenance of his airplane. I've been here ever since and am now the manager of Carnmore Airport.

In 1974, the company offered to share the facilities here with Aer Araan. Aer Araan is an airline that was founded in the late 1960s to provide a service between the Aran Islands and the mainland. They operate four "Islander" planes, ferrying Aran residents and tourists across the water. Before the service started, the only way of traveling to the islands was by boat, and that journey could take three hours, even on a calm day.

The Aran Islands are a small group at the entrance to Galway Bay. There are three main islands, called, in English, Inishmore, Inishmaan and Inisheer. About

1,000 people live on the Aran Islands: most of them are crofters and weavers, although a few small electronics factories have recently started production there.

Since 1974, I have built up Carnmore into the fourth-busiest airport in Eire. About 40,000 passengers come through here every year, most of them tourists who want to visit the islands. Local businesses, however, also use the airport, and the government has recently pledged I£1.2 million ($1.5 million) for the upgrading of the runway and the provision of landing lights, a new terminal building and a navigation tower.

The future of Carnmore looks very exciting. We are all looking forward to the time when this airport, which was once a tiny, unlit grass strip, becomes a busy international airport.

John discusses a technical point with one of his pilots at Carnmore.

Dry stone walls, built of limestone, are characteristic features of the Aran Islands.

"We make the best butter in Europe"

Finbarr McLoughlin is 41. He is the general manager of Virginia Milk Products, who, together with Gilbey Distillers, have been making Bailey's Irish Cream Liqueur since 1973.

Ireland is known throughout the world as a dairying nation. We have a long history of making the best butter in Europe and we export as much cheese as New Zealand. About ten years ago, however, there was talk among the dairy farmers of switching to a cash crop or concentrating on beef. In short, we were at a crossroads and had to make a decision.

We had joined the EEC in 1973 and by the mid-Seventies, we were contributing to the enormous European butter mountain, while watching our markets dwindle. It was at this time that the idea of mixing two of the most well-known Irish products was suggested. So it was that cream and Irish whiskey came together in the same bottle. We called the mixture Bailey's Irish Cream Liqueur.

With careful advertising and rigid production control, the liqueur began to take off. Although this firm was at the forefront of cream liqueur development, many other companies have since started selling a product similar to ours. Bailey's, however, is still probably the most successful of them all. We now use 175 million liters (38 million gallons) of milk a year to produce about 40 million bottles of liqueur.

We have our milk delivered from farms within a 95-kilometer (60-mile) radius of here. There are about 4,000 farmers who regularly supply us. We have a fleet of forty-five tankers to collect the milk and employ 100 people at the factory.

Our main problem is the seasonal variation in the milk supply. Most farms produce about ten times as much milk in June as in December. The average herd of dairy cattle in Ireland numbers only twenty-one animals, and sixty percent of all herds comprise less than forty cows. This means that milk production is based on summer grass, as most farmers cannot afford to supplement the cows' feeding through the winter months.

Of the 5,100 million liters (1,120 million gallons) of milk produced in Ireland every year, more than ninety percent of it is processed into dairy products. About seventy

percent goes to make butter, cheese and yogurt; we use ten percent of it to make cream liqueur, and the rest is turned into milk powder.

We eat a lot of dairy products in Ireland – about twice as much as any other EEC country. Further research is being done all the time to find ways of utilizing our surplus resources. Maybe one day some-

Ireland's dairy herds are famous throughout the world.

one will even come up with an idea as good as Bailey's, but I don't think anything could taste as good.

Finbarr discusses a problem with his firm's production manager.

"Smuggling is a constant problem for us"

Wilhelmina Hefferlan is 23. She was born in Coventry, England, but grew up in Dublin. She works as a customs official on the border with Northern Ireland at Carrickarnon, near Dundalk.

After I had done my initial training with the Customs and Excise Department, I was sent to a place called Pettigoe, in County Donegal. I was there for fourteen months and although the winters in that part of Ireland are very cold, I soon came to enjoy living out in the country. The customs post was very small and there was hardly any traffic coming or going across the border. I worked with one other officer there and we both became very much part of the community. We had lots of friends in the village and we soon got to know all the drivers who used the route to cross into the North.

I have now been transferred to the border post at Carrickarnon. This is one of the busiest crossing points between Northern Ireland and Eire, so we have a continuous flow of lorries (trucks), coaches (buses) and cars. I work a shift system here with fifteen other uniformed officers and seven administrative staff, who check documents and customs declarations.

My job is to see that people don't exceed the limits of goods allowed across the border, as laid down in the EEC regulations. Most goods are cheaper in Northern Ireland, so there is a great temptation for our people to come back into the country with more than they are allowed. The regulations are very complicated, but generally, if any single item is worth more than I£55

Wilhelmina checks another car as it passes through the customs post.

($70), duty should be paid on it. Furthermore, there is a limit as to how much petrol (gasoline), alcohol and tobacco can be brought into Eire.

There are over 150 road crossings between the north and south which have no regular customs patrol. The amount of smuggling done across the border using these roads is a constant problem for us. The driver of a vehicle carrying taxable goods who wants to use an "unapproved" crossing, should really contact our department, so that one of our mobile units can inspect his vehicle. In practice, however, this rarely happens, because most lorries use the main road routes, on which there are permanent posts, and anyone with anything to hide will, of course, not be over-keen to get in touch with us.

When I'm off duty I play a lot of sport. I live in Dundalk now and the sports facilities here are very good, with a swimming pool, sports center and lots of squash courts. My boyfriend is also a keen sportsman. He often takes part in amateur motor-racing events and we always go to the small town of Ballyjamesduff in County Cavan for the racing. Every year the village streets are turned into a race-track for one weekend in June. Grandstands are built overnight and hundreds of hay bales are stacked against walls and around lamp posts. There are races for Formula Ford and rally cars. Unfortunately, my boyfriend didn't do very well this year: he crashed his car on the second lap of the first race!

The motor-racing at Ballyjamesduff has become an annual event.

"Cork may become a second Aberdeen"

Derek Lehane is 18 and still at school. During his vacations and on weekends he has what is probably the most unusual job in the whole of Eire: he helps visitors kiss the famous Blarney Stone.

I live in Cork, the second largest city in Eire. It was founded by the Vikings on an island in the Lee River over 1,000 years ago, and now 150,000 people live here. Being on an island, Cork has a great number of bridges, linking the city with the banks of the river. In 1920, British troops set fire to parts of the city, but these areas have been rebuilt and Cork now has a modern commercial center, with good facilities for young and old.

Gas and oil have recently been discovered off Kinsale Head, which is just to the south of here. In 1982, the Irish Gas Board built a pipeline from Cork to Dublin and this has brought a lot more employment to the region. Some say that Cork may even become a second Aberdeen.

The gas and oil industry is unlikely, however, to take over from the tourist industry in Eire. Although we are primarily a farming nation, tourism is now our

Derek helps another tourist kiss the famous Blarney Stone.

third largest industry after agriculture and manufacturing. Eire now earns nearly I£1 billion ($1.26 billion) a year from tourism. When visitors first began to arrive here in the late nineteenth century, most of them came from Britain. Now they come from all over the world, and the United States has taken over from Britain as the country which gives us the greatest revenue from tourism.

The tourists' favorite haunt is Killarney in County Kerry, with its lakes and mountains, but Blarney Castle, just north of Cork, runs it a close second. The present-day castle is the third to have been built on the same site. The first was built of wood in the tenth century, but was replaced by a stone structure in 1210. The castle was extended in 1446 and since then, it has changed little.

Blarney Castle is famous for the Blarney Stone. This is a huge slab of rock set into the battlements high up on the keep. Some say that the stone was given to the then king of Ireland by Robert the Bruce, as a present for lending him 4,000 troops when he fought the Battle of Bannockburn. Others tell of how the stone was given to the king by a witch that he had saved from drowning. She told him that anyone who kissed the stone would be granted the gift of eloquence. That is the reason why visitors kiss the stone even to this day.

It's a long climb up a spiral stairway to get to the top of the keep. The Blarney Stone protrudes out over the side of the battlements and it is quite difficult to reach without help. That's where I come in. I hold the visitors' waists as they lie on their backs and, with the aid of two iron handholds, lean out and kiss the stone. It is not the easiest task in the world, and some people get into some very strange positions. I've been working here for about four years during my school vacations and on weekends.

Blarney Castle, near Cork, is high on the list of attractions for most visitors.

"Craftsmen were recruited from all over Europe"

Tom Kirby is 51. He works as one of 700 glass cutters employed at Waterford Crystal Limited in the historic town of Waterford, 130 km (80 miles) south of Dublin. His son has recently begun working at the factory too.

A selection of work produced by Waterford Crystal Limited.

My son completes his five-year apprenticeship as a glass cutter this year. It will be a proud day for me and for him. I began working here in 1950 and served a five-year apprenticeship, just like my son. I learned the trade from a German who was employed here after the war; my son was taught by me.

Although Waterford Crystal Limited is now a large and flourishing company, employing over 3,000 people, it has had its share of past misfortune. Founded in 1783 by George and William Penrose, the company soon came to be associated with high-quality glass. However, by 1851, high wages and heavy duties on the imported raw materials had forced the company to close down.

Luckily, all was not lost. In 1950, Joseph McGrath, a well-known fighter for Irish independence, took over the company name and Waterford Crystal Limited was reborn — ninety-nine years after its initial closure. A new factory was built and experienced craftsmen were recruited from all over Europe.

Making finished lead crystal involves a number of careful and intricate processes. These begin with the selection of high-quality raw materials. We import silica sand from Belgium, lead from Australia and potash from Germany. All the ingredients are melted in special clay pots which we import from England. They are heated to 1,400° Celsius (2552°F) and are kept at that temperature for thirty-six hours, before the glass is ready for refining and, eventually, blowing.

The blower's job is probably the best known in the industry. He takes a long, hollow tube and dips it into the molten glass, gathering a blob on the end. He then blows through the tube to form a bubble. The exact shape of the piece is determined by a water-cooled wooden mold in which the glass is placed. Although the master blower performs the actual shaping of the glass, he is just one of a team involved in the whole production process.

When the glass is cool, it comes to our department for cutting. It is cut with carborundum wheels. The wheels are fixed to benches and the glass is held up to them as they spin, thus scoring the surface and making the "cut." This company is famous for its variety of designs; among its most well-known are honeycombs of diamonds, bands of diamonds, and strawberry inserts and flutings.

Cutting is a highly skilled job and there is no easy route to being the best: you just have to work at it for years. It can take weeks to complete the cutting of just one piece. This is not surprising, however, when you consider that a single item can sell for as much as I£5,000 ($6,000). All our glass is stamped with our name, but the connoisseur doesn't need to look for the mark: he can tell if a piece is ours just by the feel of it.

Tom has worked on some of the most intricate pieces made by the company.

"Fish farming is becoming a big business in Eire"

Marion Cunningham is 43. She was born in Guildford, England, but now lives with her husband and their five children in Killarney, County Kerry, where they run a small restaurant.

I was born in Guildford, where twenty years ago I met and married an Irishman from Dublin. He eventually persuaded me to come and live in Ireland, and we moved to a small village called Dingle, on the west coast of County Kerry.

My husband started his own woodcarving business, producing small, lathe-turned ornaments that he sold to the thousands of tourists who flock to the Dingle Peninsula every year. Things were going well and we soon had enough money to open a restaurant. I did all the cooking myself and we employed a couple of part-timers to serve at table and wash the dishes.

In the past, Dingle was a simple fishing village, renowned for its beautiful scenery. To the south lies the picturesque Dingle Bay and to the north is Mount Brandon, a peak named after St. Brendon, who, the Irish claim, discovered the Americas

Marion prepares dinner for her guests: a dish of locally caught shellfish.

in the sixth century A.D., long before Columbus. The beauty of the place has attracted more and more visitors and now the locals derive most of their income, not from the sea, but from the countless tourists who flock to the village.

The lack of customers in winter, however, persuaded us to move our business to Killarney. Like Dingle, Killarney boasts many restaurants; there must be close to one hundred in the town. However, unlike Dingle, it has a sizeable resident population of about 14,000, so even in the middle of winter, there is a chance that we will be half-full.

Killarney is probably the best known of all the towns in Kerry. It has been one of the world's most famous beauty spots for centuries. Built on the shores of a lake and surrounded by mountains, it offers the tourist everything from luxury hotels to boat trips and mountaineering. Across the lake from the town are Macgillicuddy's Reeks, a mountain range of sandstone and volcanic rock. One of the peaks, Carraun-toohil, stands 1,041 m (3,414 ft) high, making it the highest mountain in the whole of Ireland.

We can seat up to forty people in our restaurant, which we have called "Dingles" in memory of the happy times we had in that village. We serve all kinds of food, but always make sure the menu includes some traditional local dishes, like Irish stew or poached fresh salmon.

Our fish come from the rivers, lakes and sea around Kerry. Fish farming is becoming a big business in Eire, especially the rearing of shellfish and salmon. Salmon fry are reared in huge wire cages suspended in the bays around the coast. This business is still at the experimental stage, but it is hoped that with proper management, salmon farming will boom here as it has in Norway. Then everyone will perhaps be able to afford the luxury of poached or smoked salmon.

The lakes of Killarney are internationally renowned for their beauty.

"Drugs were a big problem in Dublin"

Dermot Mann is 25. He lives in Dublin and has been a member of the *Garda Siochana* (the Irish Police Force) for five years. He is based at Foley Street Police Station, the largest one in Dublin.

I grew up on the streets of Dublin, and I now patrol them as a *garda*, or policeman. The Irish Police Force is called the *Garda Siochana*, which literally translated means "the Guardians of the Peace." The force was set up in 1922, after the Anglo-Irish Treaty of 1921 made Eire a dominion of the British Commonwealth. We are now a national force of 11,400 officers, of whom 350 are women. Like our British counterparts, we don't carry firearms, except in special circumstances.

The national force is split into twenty-three divisions, each headed by a chief superintendent. The country is further divided into forty districts, each of which is overseen by a superintendent. The number of police stations in a district varies according to the size of the district and its population. In some of Eire's most remote regions, there are even one-man police stations responsible for fairly large areas of the country.

Although Dublin is a small city by world standards (there are only 915,000 people

Dermot and a colleague patrol the busy Dublin streets.

living here), it is the center of government, and therefore requires special policing. Politicians, generals and diplomats all have to be protected, and this makes heavy demands on the *Garda Siochana*.

We have recently had a fairly severe problem with teenage vandalism, which can be partly put down to the lack of employment opportunities here in the capital. There was a time when young people, most of them boys of about 14 or 15, would pinch cars and go joy riding. It got so bad that they would even drive to the police station and hoot until we chased them! These chases often ended in accidents, so eventually, we decided to simply ignore the youths until they drove off. This had the desired effect and since then, fewer cars have been stolen.

Drugs, especially heroin, were also a big problem in Dublin. Much of the heroin used to come in through the port, but with careful and strict patrolling, we have now got the situation under control and the drug problem is no longer growing at the rate it was. There is a very strong family feeling in Eire and in these cases of drug abuse, we have always tried to involve the offenders' families in the matter, because we cannot rehabilitate the youngsters without their help. This emphasis on the family is as strong in Dublin today as it was 200 years ago. Our whole society is held together by family ties.

The *Garda Siochana* have recently introduced a Juvenile Liaison Scheme, whereby young offenders are dealt with by a specially trained officer. This means that the problem can often be sorted out on a one to one basis and the youths need not have a police record. This system seems to be working well, and it is strengthening the relationship between the police and the community. It is also helping to keep the crime rate under control.

Modern vehicles and equipment help the Garda *in their fight against crime.*

"We found everything we had dreamed of"

Joseph Zimmerman is 42 and was born in West Germany. He now lives with his family on Achill Island, off the coast of County Mayo, where he works as a deck hand on a fishing boat.

I was born in Düsseldorf, in Germany, where I lived until 1979. I was doing well in my job as a computer systems analyst, but I wasn't really content with my life. I had been to Eire with some of my friends in 1975, when we came for the sea angling here on the west coast. I wondered then what life would be like for myself and my family if we were to move over here. When I returned to the hectic, cut-throat world of Düsseldorf, I told my wife about Eire. I told her all about the beauty and tranquility of the country, and about the genuine, friendly people. Ten months later, we had moved to Achill Island.

Achill Island is one of the areas that make up the *Gaeltacht*, the Irish-speaking part of Eire. Most of the *Gaeltacht* regions are on the west coast. Up until the sixteenth century, a far greater part of Ireland was Irish-speaking, but with the coming of the Land Tenure Act, the landowners began conducting their business in English. The Irish language fell into decline. It has, however, been preserved

The processing for export of locally caught fish is a growing industry on Achill.

The fishing boats are regularly brought up onto the beach to be cleaned.

and jealously guarded by those living in the *Gaeltacht*. They speak Irish as their first language, even though most of them can speak English too.

When we first arrived here, there was no work for me. As you can imagine, there is little demand for computer analysts on Achill. Luckily, fishing has always been a part of life here and I have always been a keen sea angler, so I was eventually able to get a job with one of the local fishermen. I've worked for him ever since.

Many species of fish are found in Ireland's waters. The most common are cod, haddock, skate, plaice, herring, mackerel, whiting and dogfish. Although fishing has always been a major source of income here on the west coast, Irish waters have not attracted the mass trawling that is typical of Scottish waters, for instance. Although our resources are very rich, the *Bord Iascaigh Mhara* (Sea Fisheries Board) control the number of licenses issued to fishermen very strictly. They are also extremely keen to protect our waters from foreign trawlers. The country's annual catch averages about 193,000 tons of seafood, most of which is exported. The export of fish is worth about I£50 million ($63 million) to our economy.

Our lives here are so different from the ones we left behind in Germany. We have to work hard just to survive, not to buy a bigger car. It is often hard to make ends meet, but our lives are always full, our days are never the same and our children are always smiling.

"Gaelic games have become popular with youngsters"

Paddy Kelly is 30. He works as a science and physical education teacher in a Christian Brothers school in Tipperary, but lives in Kilmallock, County Limerick. When he is not teaching, he plays hurling, a sport unique to Ireland.

I've been a teacher since 1976 and now work at a Christian Brothers school in Tipperary town, where I teach science and physical education.

Sport is very important to most Irish people, and although our facilities are not always wonderful, we get the best out of what we have.

Hurling is probably the game that most foreigners associate with Ireland. Played with a broad, curved stick, similar to a hockey stick, it is regarded by many people as the fastest and most skilful of all ball-and-stick games.

The modern game is played by two teams of fifteen people each, on a field similar in size to a soccer field. At each end are the goal posts, which are about 6m (20ft) apart and 6m (20ft) high, with a crossbar at 3m (10ft). Goals which count for three points, are scored when the ball is driven between the posts and under the

Limerick, in southwestern Ireland, is a major center of Gaelic sports.

crossbar, while a single point is recorded if the ball passes between the posts and over the crossbar. The side with the greatest number of points after sixty minutes wins the game.

Although I am a full-time teacher, I also play hurling for County Limerick. I play in a position called left half forward, which means I have a midfield attacking role. The Limerick team plays all over Ireland, although the top league teams are mostly to be found in the south and southwest of the country. Each year we compete with the other county teams to reach the All Ireland Final, which is played at Croke Park in Dublin.

Croke Park is the largest sports stadium in the whole of Ireland, with a capacity of 72,000. It is also the headquarters of the GAA, the Gaelic Athletic Association. All members of the GAA are amateurs, which

Hurling is regarded as the fastest of all ball-and-stick games.

means that we are not paid for playing sport. Our reward is a sense of personal satisfaction and achievement, and the knowledge that we are promoting a truly Irish game.

The rules of Gaelic soccer are in many respects similar to those of hurling, although it is played with a bigger ball and the players have no sticks. It is a bit like soccer, except that the players are allowed to pick the ball up and run with it. Points are scored in exactly the same way as in hurling.

Over the past few years, Gaelic games have become so popular with youngsters that the country is now desperately short of good facilities for teaching and promoting our national sports.

"We are the largest shipping company in Eire"

Frank Forde is 55, married and has four sons. He is the captain of the M. V. *Connaught*, one of the six passenger ferries belonging to Ireland's state-owned B & I Line.

I come from Arklow, a small town on the coast of County Wicklow, south of Dublin. It is often said that "everyone in Arklow is a sailor," so I suppose it's not really surprising that I'm a ferry captain! Like all boys in Arklow, I wanted to go away to sea from the moment I first thought about a job. I eventually succeeded at the age of 15, when I joined the Irish Shipping Line as a deck hand. By 1951 I had been round the world, having visited Australia, New Zealand, Canada, the United States and the West Indies.

In 1952 the British and Irish Steam Packet Company were advertising for officers for their boats, so I applied for a job with them. They offered me a position as a second mate and I began working on their container fleet, trading between Ireland and the major European ports. Then in 1965 I became a captain. For the following three years, I continued to work the European routes, but when I was 38 I got married and, by coincidence, the company purchased their first drive-on ferry in the

Frank takes the controls of the M.V. Connaught *as she comes into Dublin.*

same year. They offered me the captaincy of the ship and I accepted.

This company began life in 1836, carrying passengers and freight to Britain. In 1965 the Irish Government took over the

A B & I ferry takes on passengers in the busy port of Dublin.

operation, which is now one hundred percent government-owned. The ship of which I am now the captain, the M.V. *Connaught*, was bought in 1979. Built by the Verolme Cork Dockyard, the M.V. *Connaught* is one of two 7,500-ton vessels owned by the company. She, and her sister ship, the M.V. *Leinster*, are each capable of carrying as many as 1,500 passengers and 350 cars.

There are 106 crew on board my ship, the majority of them catering staff. We are based at the B & I Port in Dublin, a 16-hectare (40-acre) complex at the center of the largest industrial estate in Ireland. My ship sails daily to Liverpool or Holyhead, while other B & I ferries sail to Fleetwood,

Rotterdam, Antwerp and Le Havre from Dublin, and to Pembroke from Rosslare.

Each year, B & I Ferries transport 1.1 million passengers and over 150,000 cars, not to mention the 2.2 million tons of cargo we handle annually. We are the largest shipping company in Eire and employ about 1,700 people in various capacities. We have staff operating package holidays all over the Continent, as well as within our own country. All these things add up to making us the largest carrier between Britain and the Irish Republic, accounting for more than one-third of the total trade.

I have four sons and one of them is very interested in becoming a seaman. I can only hope that he gets the chance to have as good an education in the job as I had when I was younger, and trust that he too can one day work for B & I Ferries.

Facts

Capital city: Dublin (population about 900,000).

Languages: Irish and English are the two official languages.

Currency: The Irish pound, or *punt*, in which there are 100 *pighne* (pence). There is approximately .79 *punt* to $1.00 U.S.

Religion: About ninety-five percent of the population belong to the Roman Catholic Church, the remainder being mainly members of the Protestant Church of Ireland. There are also small numbers of Jews.

Population: In 1982, there were 3,480,000 people living in the Republic of Ireland. Approximately half of them live in Leinster Province, which covers a large area of eastern and central Ireland.

Climate: Warm, moist air from the Atlantic Ocean means that much of Ireland, and the west coast in particular, experiences fairly mild winters. The average winter temperature is as high as 7°C (44°F), on the west coast, dropping to 5°C (41°F) in the east. Summers are warm but fairly wet and many parts of the country have an annual rainfall of over 100cm (40 inches).

Government: The President is head of the Irish State. He is elected for a seven-year term by all citizens of the republic. The President officially appoints the Prime Minister (*Taoiseach*) but only on the nomination of the *Dáil*. *Dáil Éireann* is the lower house of the Irish Parliament; made up of 144 representatives, it alone can initiate parliamentary bills. *Seanad Éirann*, the upper house of Parliament, cannot stop legislation, but may amend it. The Government of the country is made up of around ten to fifteen members, usually drawn from Dáil Éireann.

Housing: Since World War II, Ireland's housing has been modernized extensively. Public housing is commissioned by local councils and paid for with grants from Central Government. There is also a fair amount of private construction in some areas.

Education: Elementary, or first-level schools are free to all children between the ages of 6 and 15. They must attend either state-funded or private schools. Many private schools in Eire are run by various Roman Catholic Orders, some of which receive support from Central Government. Secondary schools are also free, and teach a varied curriculum. Irish is a major subject and in some schools, all classes are conducted in Irish.

Agriculture: Agriculture accounts for eleven percent of Ireland's gross domestic product. Milk and dairy products are produced in large quantities, very often for export. Potatoes, Ireland's traditional agricultural product, are no longer farmed on such a large scale; many farmers have diversified into green vegetables, sugar beet and various cash crops.

Industry: Ireland's earliest industry was the textile and weaving trade, which has, however, declined in the twentieth century. Other traditional businesses, such as brewing, fertilizer production, and canning, are mainly carried out through small established concerns. New overseas investment has recently widened the industrial production of Ireland and there has been a growth in the manufacture of a wide range of consumer products, from basic foodstuffs to electronic appliances. Reserves of gas and oil have also begun to be exploited in the south of the country.

Media: Ireland has four national daily newspapers and a wide range of provincial and periodical publications. *Radio Telefis Eiraan* (RTE) is the country's one broadcasting service, transmitting television programs on two channels. There are three different radio channels, one of which is an all-Irish service.

Glossary

Bog An area of wet ground in which dead leaves and plants rot, and eventually form peat.

Cash Crop Any crop which is grown to be sold rather than used directly.

Crofter Someone who farms a small area of land, especially in Ireland or Scotland.

Dominion The name given to self-governing regions of the British Empire.

EEC European Economic Community; official name for the Common Market, an economic association created to abolish barriers to free trade among member nations.

Gaelic Relating to the Celtic peoples of Scotland and Eire.

Gaeltacht Those areas of Ireland in which the Irish language is still commonly used.

Hopper A large container in which solid materials can be stored.

Hot Metal A printing method in which molten metal is molded into individual letters and then remelted after use.

Itinerant Traveling from place to place.

Lead Crystal High-quality transparent glass.

Peat A compacted brown substance which forms when dead leaves and plants rot in water.

Single transferable vote A vote that can count for a second candidate if the voter's first choice is eliminated in an election.

Swallow holes Holes in the ground down which running water flows.

Teachdaí Dála Irish parliament member.

Index